ALLIF DOVE

Unity – God – Success

Let's Make It Happen America!

GLORY RELEASE GLOBAL

Contents

Preface

One thing I know for sure is I am called to write this book. Why? I don't know? Who will read it? I'm not sure. Is it pertinent? Certainly, I think so. Will it help? Sincerely hope so. What's it all about? Well since the presidential election of 2008 America has admittedly been seeking change. The automotive, financial and housing industries were in shambles. In fact the United States government took over management of one of its largest car manufacturers. There were cries about government interference. Words like apathy, mismanagement, arrogance, waste and greed continuously swirled, stirred, settled and then swirled again. A new administration settled in, working consistently, shooting for progress and at the same time field questions, rendered replies and absorbed criticism. After all, what else can they do in a country whose doctrine says, the elected officials answer to its citizens while the citizens reserve the right to rationalize, analyze and criticize as they see fit.

Now, more than a decade into this century we see technology at its highest heights while morality, based on daily news accounts, seems to be at the lowest of lows. Someone once said "It ain't over until the fat lady sings" but I subscribe to Yogi Berra's rendition which says "It ain't over until it's over"! How about that? We still have time to develop a method, put forth effort and muster the much-needed consistency for progress and permanent change.

As with any recovery process a vision of where we want and need to go is necessary. But of greater significance is finding out where we came from and how we got here. And equally as critical is our plan for positive change. As you read, I do hope you consider the many issues prevalent in our society such as finances, youth, education, lack of employment, addiction, sexual and race issues, foreclosure, corruption, foreign affairs and criminal activity all of which tend to result in frustration, aggravation, separation and a seeming state of annihilation. Many books address solutions to issues. This book aims at the ingredients, method and art of positive change. In nontraditional form I will utilize a series of personal poems, essays, articles, commentaries and editorials to share these ideas. Our country's founding principles when accepted and applied seem to always place us on solid footing. Many recognize the need for unity in preserving our beloved country. And thus, with that in mind, is it safe to say, "let us put our best foot forward"?

Introduction

As I write this introduction, I am amazed at how much my mindset has changed since I wrote the preface over a year ago. At that time, I felt I had something to say and it was good and it sounded good. Mighty egotistical of me, with such thinking, as I reflect on it today. Since then, I remember a man I became acquainted with through my job. This man was a writer and in particular he wrote plays. After speaking with him one day about some of his finished work, our conversation shifted slightly to who he envisioned his intended audience to be. Nevertheless, the most precious information I felt I gained from the conversation was how this man was adamant about the fact that an artist should be honored and grateful that someone gave them their valuable attention out of their valuable time.

As a result of this conversation, I am truly aware that any attention a reader gives this book should be greatly appreciated by me. I truly thank God because I feel these articles, essays and poems I have offered, along with commentary regarding the principles I believe support them, can and will add to the healing of America. Today as I sit, look, work, watch and listen it becomes increasingly evident that the days are evil but thanks be to God that He stands for the opposite (spelled backward) of the word evil which is the word *live*. And according to the bible God not only wants us to live, he wants us to live abundantly.

In this book you will come to see several common themes which are namely the benefit of our collective and purposeful efforts (Unity), the source for accomplishing this (GOD) and the desired outcome for any sane American (Success) from which the title of this book comes. Unity– GOD – Success; Let's Make it Happen America.

I

1. Determination

de·ter·mi·na·tion
noun

Firmness of purpose; resoluteness.

Principle: Determination

As I commuted to work on Wednesday November 5, 2008, the atmosphere on the bus seemed to be pleasant but dazed. History had been made and it was less than 24 hours old. Some people openly verbalized their happiness about America's newest choice to serve as President of the United States of America. Just one day before many people had endured long lines and sacrificed their day, to play a role in this selection.

America's people had made a concerted and determined effort to change some things. There had been a platform encouraging change, and change had occurred indeed. In true form the majority of voting Americans had changed their minds and their actions followed.

This was truly a memorable moment for America and the world. It spoke volumes about getting involved, getting educated about how things work and the responsibility that each American citizen has in making sound decisions about who they select to represent them. It evoked hope in African-Americans and all other minority groups about what can be achieved with effort and determination. The 2008 presidential election spoke volumes about America's image as a land of opportunity. There are surely more benefits that resulted from this historical moment, but there is one area of profound impact. The election of Barack Obama as the 44th president of the United States of America sent a profound message to the world about the value of Democracy and what makes Democracy work in its purest form.

As I wrote the following short commentary ("A New Day") about this moment in American history, what stuck out most to me was the determination of the American citizens. They were simply looking for the best candidate they could find. This is what makes Democracy work best. This is what opens man up to the power of God. This has marked the beginning of "A New Day" in American politics. As you read this essay I hope you can remember the determination of the people. People who spent time reading, speaking out, writing and listening; people who were determined to ensure a government that serves its people and their needs.

Finally included in this chapter on determination are two letters ("Best Ram Ever– Mr. Football" and "Good Thing For A Decent Person") that highlight the efforts of two of America's most successful athletes in their respective sports. Their determination is clearly seen by all who have witnessed their performances but of greater value they serve as evidence of what can be achieved when we embody such a quality.

* * *

A New Day

Luther Vandross once sang "The sun is shining, there's plenty of light, and a new day is dawning, sunny and bright." And that's America today. What a wonderful night it was on Tuesday November 4, 2008 when our country did as Spike Lee might say "the right thing." We as a people resolutely looked past color, gender, age, race, etc and decided to pick the candidate that represented himself as the best executive to lead us out of tough times to say the least. What a decision! WOW! Outstanding!

Almost as outstanding that same night was President elect Barack Obama's speech, during which he verbally committed to lead this country back to the ways our forefathers envisioned. Yes, he committed to lead and not to dominate or, of greater importance not to mislead us, which seems to have been the case for some time now. It was an elegantly expressed speech which effectively reminded us that this government is "for the people, by the people."

Yes, it was a new day when these newly motivated people, inspired by so many events over the last eight years, purposed to make a statement, endured long lines and finally said with a vote "enough is enough and too much stinks." I suppose we should surely thank God (In whom we trust) for his grace during a time when many of our actions were less than responsible. And thanks President elect Obama for congratulating us last night but also for reminding us – We have more work to do! John F. Kennedy is known for saying "Ask not what your country can do for you, but what you can do for your country" and on Tuesday November 4, 2008 the people of the United States of America took its first step towards doing exactly that.

We were asked by our newly elected president to re-commit to re-unify to re-establish our core values to strengthen our beloved country.

So on each day,
Can we commit to stay?
Committed that day,
To the American way,
Like we were...On Election Day!

Allif Dove
11/5/2008

* * *

Best Ram Ever — Mr. Football

Thanks St. Louis American for your article "Best Ram ever" written by Mike Claiborne on Mr. Marshall Faulk last week. I would simply like to add the following.

Once in a while there comes along a person who truly deserves to be called "The Best." Such a player is not only outstanding in their position, but because of the tenacity, vigor, dedication and determination they bring to the game, it can be reasonably imagined that they could excel at several other positions at football's highest level (National Football League – NFL).

In my opinion, of course, Mr. Marshall Faulk could surely have excelled as a wide receiver, defensive back and a kick returner and perhaps an outside linebacker or maybe even a quarterback. Yet in spite of what other positions he could have played, the very position he did play was thoroughly revolutionized by his accomplishments. Yes there have been outstanding running backs that could run, block and catch but few possessed the total package like Mr. Faulk.

Thus, for his passion, consistency, intellect and football presence and most of all his ability to infect or affect teammates to play the same way, he should be on a short NFL list of the greatest football players of all time.

Congratulations Hall of Famer, Mr. Marshall Faulk for leaving it all on the field and for a career well executed. And knowing you, I believe the best has yet to come.

Allif Dove
August 8, 2011

* * *

Good Thing For A Decent Person

During a time in America when hearing bad news was routine, it was surely a pleasurable moment when Derek Jeter of the New York Yankees went down and roped a low pitch high over the left field fence for his 3000th hit. What a way to go over an exceptional mark with a bang!

What makes this all the more awesome is it could not have happened to a more productive, exemplary and deserving individual. Mr. Jeter, and I say Mr., has proceeded to consistently work hard, play hard and be a solid leader in a time when such longevity is becoming rarely heard of. He is a credit to his family, the New York Yankees, Major League baseball and the United States of America.

Truly a good thing has happened to one who has carried himself in a decent and admirable way. And there is no secret how it happened because many of us have witnessed how he got his success. He got it the old fashion way. He earned it (no steroids). So all I can say is God bless Mr. Jeter and I hope to see many young Americans use his example of determination as a source of inspiration to achieve such excellence. Kudos to Mr. Jeter!

Allif Dove
July 10, 2011

* * *

II

2. Honesty

hon·es·ty
noun

Adherence to the facts and quality of being honest.

Principle: Honesty

Over the years, working as a Human Service professional in many capacities, I have and still do engage many people who arrive in our program with a desire to change their situation. They no longer want the type of results they have been getting. They are fed up at least with their pain. A part of my job is to help them see how bad things really are and what role, actions they took, they played in getting where they are in life. The previous chapter talked about the determination of America's people with regard to wanting a change but now comes time to probe and when it comes to probing an essential tool is honesty.

I like to refer to this essential tool as "Ground Zero." This is primarily because all positive change relies on a sobering or realistic analysis of the state of affairs as they really are. Professionals like doctors, mechanics or plumbers, all of which engage in taking corrective actions, know that before something can be fixed it must be diagnosed. This diagnosis must be accurate to enable the repairer to devise a course of action.

In this chapter, I begin with a poem "Shootings, Stop It" which captures the current state in our society concerning this critical issue, "guns". This is followed by another poem, "Enough", which I believe is the silent cry of many citizens when they hear about tragedy after tragedy. And finally, this chapter concludes with an essay entitled "Ground Zero."

Of course, America's citizens had to begin at "Ground Zero" to become determined to seek a change but now, as we move toward viable solutions, the time has come to assess honestly what, why, and how things have happened and ultimately how to change our situation. It is my hope that this essay will provide insight on how to develop this tool, honesty (or truthfulness) and begin to use it routinely. This will enable each American citizen to truly acknowledge if they have fully participated in the Democratic process and if their actions have been detrimental or beneficial with regard to America's current state.

So honestly assessing the situation we are in, it is fair to say Americans possess vast access to education and information. Many have an ability to get food, clothing and shelter enabling them to at least participate in our democratic process. Thus to the degree that we honestly evaluate and determine to improve our performance, do we truly understand the fact that if America is not doing well, it is because the *Americans (as a whole) are not functioning well. Ground zero therefore is to practice honestly assessing one's own actions with regard to the welfare of our country and make improvements where necessary.*

* * *

Shootings? Stop It!

Shootings here, shootings there,
Shootings, shootings everywhere.
Shootings of children
Shootings of law enforcement officers.

Random shootings, planned shootings,
Shootings, shootings, shootings!
Shootings in schools, shootings in malls,
Shootings in movie theaters,

Shootings at political events,
Shootings in sanctuaries.
Are you kidding? What's going on?
Shootings!

Why is this happening?

Well it starts with thoughts of shootings...
"Shoot him, shoot her, and shoot them."
Thoughts and more thoughts...

"Get'em, Get'em, Get'em!"
Bang, bang, bang!
It's in their thinking.
What can we do?

Yet while we think...
Boom, boom, boom!
More shootings.
What can we do?

Change their thinking...
To change their actions.
But how?

All I know is we must stop the shootings.
Stop it!

Allif Dove, an American Writer
"We Can Do It With God's Help"

* * *

Enough

Someone once said enough *is* enough.
That same one said, and too much stinks.
I like the sayings, when the going gets tough,
The tough get going.

And if you are going to do something,
May as well do it right.
But if you can't do it right,
Then maybe you shouldn't do it at all.

But if you chose to do it,
Then maybe you can get some help
Because people like their stuff
Done right,

Even if it takes all night.

And if you don't get it right
There could be a big fight.
But if it is at all possible,

Before fixing things seems impossible,
Maybe you can gather your thought,
Recognize enough *is* enough,
Hang in there and be tough,

Then come up with a plan,
To work together hand in hand,
And avoid the old saying
That enough *is* enough
And too much stinks!

Allif Dove
Written about the state of America following
President Barack H. Obama Re-election
November 10, 2012

* * *

Ground Zero

Throughout the ages there have been many addictions that have trapped individuals, costing major problems within families and society or costing them to live their lives out in devastating conditions and or costing them to lose their lives. Although nicotine, food, sex and gambling, to name a few, continue to wreak havoc in the lives of many individuals, one would be hard pressed to identify a more damaging dependency than an addiction to illicit drugs or alcohol.

I can truly attest to the fact that these substances can quickly rip through a life at a merciless rate. Most people know or at least have heard of someone whose potential was ruined or who lost their life in such a battle. For those who are still caught up or know someone who is; finding support is very important but even before support can be effective there is something the individual must do.

Most addicted people have developed character traits, that if they are to recover and enjoy a peaceful existence, they must identify their detrimental ways and work towards correction. The ability to develop honesty as a way of life is a chief component of any meaningful and lasting recovery.

Most individuals seeking recovery will usually feel over-whelmed when told they must adopt and practice honesty. Therefore it should be noted that an honest person does not simply appear one day. Honesty first requires a choice, next a commitment and finally practice.

It takes time to develop honesty. In the development process of honesty, commitment is what is necessary to help individuals stay focused. During the practice phase, which is a lifelong process, an individual should zero in on what works for them. All who truly attempt to get honest, should be careful not to fall into the trap of despair or dejection. They must remember they are engaged in a process that will one day prove very rewarding. It will result in wonderful fruit. One of the most notable fruits to materialize is peace. Peace to know what our response will be in every situation and peace to know we are doing what is right. After all, no one likes to be deceived - Not even a deceiver.

Allif H. Dove (2007)

* * *

III

3. Desire

de·sire
noun

A strong feeling of wanting to have something or wishing for something to happen.

Principle: Desire

There is an old saying that I would hear a lot when I was a child and although this saying was both very beneficial and highly motivational, I don't hear it as much today. The idea "when the going gets tough, the tough get going," can help us to seek to get on track and focus on staying on track. This idea of developing a desire to improve our situation and to succeed is a valuable one.

I can't recall ever meeting anyone who didn't want to succeed at something. Whether the desire was to find a spouse, buy a house, go to college or have a baby, the goal is the same; to succeed. And although there may be many reasons why we desire to succeed, among the most common seems to be in general the idea of achieving happiness, contentment and security.

Today's American society finds our citizens engaged in debate about what, how and why things should be done (this way or that way). Many individuals or groups propose changes that they believe will result in a happier, contented and secure America. In actuality all these (happiness, contentment and security) are more likely achievable when passion and desire are strong.

Many people tend to stay frustrated when they can't see solutions. They search for answers but fail to gain and maintain the level of desire that can lead to things getting better. Some people believe there is an answer to every problem we face while others doubt this concept. Many who believe have their faith grounded on a higher plain. This faith for many is grounded in a spiritual belief. Nevertheless, a critically important ingredient in achieving a successful outcome is to develop and maintain a strong desire.

Whether you believe this or not, if you are an American you most likely desire that America succeeds in our recovery efforts. Most Americans will readily agree they are tired of robberies, murders, kidnappings and burglaries. They are fed up with various degrees of irresponsibility, manipulation and exploitation. And although we know we can participate in improving these and other areas such as quality and affordable education and healthcare, we must admit the solution for success appears to require vast understanding.

In this chapter I offer two readings, the first is a commentary entitled, "To Stop The Violence, WE Must." This commentary highlights the condition and result of violence in our society, the yearning and desire for change and most importantly the idea that our desire can and should help us probe to find solutions. And finally, I offer a poem entitled "A Quest for Success," to conclude this chapter. From a personal standpoint I can say when I didn't know which way to turn in my life, I sought God's help in choosing direction and the direction was made clear. My desire to do better brought me into the place where I could be helped. I know for certain it helped me overcome a terrific obstacle. The words of this poem literally flowed into my mind as I sought a solution. And as an American citizen and as a country I invite anyone to consider the idea in this poem as an approach to your personal and our collective desire to succeed in achieving happiness, contentment and security.

* * *

To Stop The Violence, WE Must…

Over the weekend of June 4, 2021 through June 6, 2021, there were 8 reported killings of youth in the St. Louis Metropolitan area and of course that is way too many. And yes, something needs to be done to stop this devastating trend. One local politician, when asked how to stop the killings, talked about getting to the root cause of the problem and while I agree this could definitely help, I would add that merely identifying these causes won't solve the overall problem at hand. We must identify the source of the killing problem and adequately address the elements that lead to these senseless murders. Here are three areas of concern, which I believe we must routinely yet ruthlessly address.

Anger

The first human killing recorded in the Bible was when Cain killed his brother Abel. We read that this happened because Cain was angry and ultimately violently attacked his brother. Today our society is full of many angry people and we must first see where this anger comes from. Then we must try to help our citizens desire to seek other remedies to deal with anger and ultimately help them see how to change their angry mindset. While we all do get angry, our inability to deal with these emotions is proving to be very detrimental and deadly.

Choices

Looking at the first human killing in the Bible again, we see Cain, the killer of his brother Abel, was angry because of a choice he made. He chose to bring something to God, while his brother brought something else. Today, some of our youth choose to start using drugs and/or drinking alcohol, begin indulging in defiant behavior, move on to criminal activity and many times drop out of school. By their choices and due to their exposure in many cases, they ultimately develop bad habits, which place them at risk of being victims of violent crime, cause them to suffer serious bodily injury, psychological/emotional damage, imprisonment and yes, ultimately death. Just like Cain, many of our youth killings stem from the choices they and the adults in their lives make about how they choose to live their lives.

Guidance

Taking one final look at the circumstances surrounding the first human killing in the Bible, we see God tells Cain that his anger was unjustified and could be dealt with if he simply did the right thing. It was apparent that Cain had been given the right guidance and if he had chosen to go back, recognize what he had been taught and follow that guidance, he could get back on course. This is where we are in today's society. We know that good teaching can help one attain intellectual education and success, and because we understand this concept, it is also reasonable that we understand that the failure to educate our citizens socially (adults and youth), is causing our society to teeter on the brink of destruction and total annihilation from within.

In summary, it is clear that our society's mindset is actually the source of the violence that results in these killings, which many of us are tired of hearing about. Furthermore, it appears to be plain to see that the education and or re-education of our citizens to choose the high road and avoid the low murderous alternative must be of utmost and primary concern, if we are to overcome our anger, make good choices and guide our youth in the right way.

Allif Dove
June 8, 2021

* * *

A Quest For Success

What is this thing we call success?
And on what principles does attaining it rest?
Does honesty, willingness and doing my best,
Equal this thing that is called success?

Now teachers they teach and trainers they train,
That knowledge and experience are keys to obtain.
When choosing a field, I ponder fortune and fame,
But passion and love are keys that sustain.

Some things come easy and some are hard,
But nothing is accomplished without a start.
The journey begins in search of reward,
But peaks and valleys lead to discord.

While meditating on life's many test,

It dawned on me and I must confess.
That God has a way that will surely bless,
If only I ask and seek God's success

Allif H. Dove
By the Grace of God
On August 19, 2006

* * *

IV

4. Faith

faith
noun

Complete trust or confidence in someone or something.

Principle: Faith

When I wrote the poem "A Quest For Success" I was literally seeking success in my life. I had recently been fired from a job working at a children's home for boys. I was driving a cab with a job as a Substance Abuse Counselor on the table. I literally sat down in my backyard in Jennings, Missouri right outside the city of St. Louis and four stanzas rolled off of my pen. To me it sounded wonderful but this was too easy. I wondered if I should seek another stanza between the third and the fourth. I brain stormed for a few days and finally I concluded it was God inspired. At the time I never once applied the meaning of the poem to my own situation.

At over 40 years old but 50 still a good way off, I began to search my past. What kind of work had I done? What did I do well or what did I like doing? I came up with about six job categories I had performed throughout my life and came up with a plan to remain a cab driver for now. But thank God for friends. I discussed my findings about myself with three individuals separately and when it was over I prayed for God's help in finding my place in life. I am truly happy to say that God heard my request and I've been working in this field for the last four plus years.

I share this testimony with people today because being at a crossroad and not knowing what to do, I was amazed at how God came through. Since that decision I have had the privilege of working with many men and women who were frustrated, addicted, hurt and confused and just the thought of encouraging them to go on a little longer has been highly rewarding. And just think it all came about by seeking God's success first.

Since that day in October 2006, I have had similar situations where I was at a quandary and God directed my steps upon my request. I also have seen others, in similar situations, place their trust in God and receive wonderful results. And because I have seen such results, I know if God did it for me he will do it for you. And I also know if America first seeks God's success, we will surely be blessed!

Those who believe in the concept of "In God We Trust" see the attainment of America's solutions in God. They believe our success and favor is largely due to God and that our recovery is largely dependent on God. And who could blame a person for believing that something they have seen work can work again. At this point I would like to share two letters entitled "In God We Trust" and "Why Work Together." I also would like to share an inspirational writing entitled "Placed In God's Capable Hands" because Americans have proven to be very talented yet today, we need these abilities to be used especially for the purpose of preserving our beloved country. I hope they will help with the idea of seeking God first in our recovery efforts and allowing him to guide us to success.

* * *

In God We Trust

Printed on American money is the inscription "In God We Trust." This is a pretty self-explanatory phrase, meaning when we have done all we can do we understand that it is still up to God. It also indicates that our ways may not always be right or sufficient but we rely on God to show us the way and we believe God will guide us to success.

In a country that works to provide a system through programs to help its citizens as well as to organize movements to help other countries in need, we must still remember God is the supplier of our needs, gifts, abilities and protection. Many people argue over who God is or what His name is, but most people who believe in the concept of God would probably agree that if we as a country truly sought God to answer this question as well as our questions about social difficulties, governmental affairs and environmental issues, God will answer us.

In the news the oil spill in the Gulf of Mexico is reported on daily and when it is mentioned so are BP (British Petroleum) and President Barack Obama, but God is never or rarely mentioned. Even though we know no man can make water or oil and it's apparent each day that no man can stop it either, we still fail to openly acknowledge that it is also apparent we need God's help. And His direction to us on how to receive this help can be found in the Bible in II Chronicles 7:14 which reads "If my people, who are called by my name, shall humble themselves and pray, and seek my face, and turn from their wicked ways, then I will hear from heaven, and I will forgive their sins, and I will heal their land."

Seeking God as a last resort is not a good idea but perhaps if we seek God collectively as believers in God, then we believe we will be forgiven by God and God in turn will heal the land, since then we will really be putting our trust in God. And for starters maybe this idea "In God we trust" can be headline news.

Allif Dove
June 1, 2010

* * *

Why Work Together?

Sitting in McDonald's restaurant today at Lindbergh and Patterson, in Florissant, MO having a cup of coffee, I thought to myself life is okay but what if I couldn't enjoy the experience of dining out or other American luxuries I take for granted. Customers were eating breakfast, reading newspapers and some were peering out of the window at traffic, while the citizens in the Gulf were experiencing chaos. Then I thought about God and wondered if sometimes he uses situations to see if people will work together or fight and claw against each other. Surely God can help man with inspiration to harness the oil spill but will we cease the clamor, bickering, fighting and finger pointing so we can seek Him and hear Him.

The president and other officials have vowed to hold those responsible for the oil spill accountable for their part in this matter but we also know God holds man accountable and to be civil in this place we call civilization. Thus, we could conclude that every time we have a major issue, we don't have to draw a line in the sand. If we can collectively work to help other countries, we can collectively work to help ourselves. Will another country come to our rescue without a hidden agenda? If we don't think so then maybe we could get along and work out our differences. If perhaps one would say why work together, and to that I would say, because when it's all said and done, all we have is God and ourselves.

Allif Dove
June 16, 2010

* * *

Placed In God's Capable Hands

Sometimes I wonder why I can do certain things, while I seem helpless to do others. At times I feel completely inadequate. But it's funny that as I write these feelings, I finally realize something very important. What I realize is that I was created with certain qualities, skills and talents. And I further realize I am not so talented in other areas. But nevertheless without God (talent or no talent) it's all the same. So today, I pledge to put all my abilities and inabilities in God's capable hands, because I know, with God, talents get better and rough areas (no talent) become smooth. I now know that I may never become a nuclear scientist or a chemical engineer but as long as I walk hand in hand with God I can become adequate in areas where I am weak and great in areas where God intended for me to make a difference. For without Him weak areas become weaker and strong areas are reduced to a waste.

Give God all of you and watch what he does.

Allif Dove
May 13, 2000

* * *

V

5. Commitment

com·mit·ment
noun

**The state or quality of being dedicated to a cause,
activity, etc.**

Principle: Commitment

There is no doubt that this period of American History is one of the most challenging we have ever experienced. The Revolutionary war, the Civil war, Prohibition, the Great Depression and the Civil Rights movement of the 1950's and 1960's , to name a few, are among the most challenging times in our history. Nevertheless, our current social state backed by our moral state backed by our quality of education is at an all time low.

Disrespect, disloyalty and violence has become every day, all day news. Sounds of the "What's Going On" anthem, sung by Marvin Gaye are ever so fitting today also. And while I can go on with more saga, I think it is fitting to share a published letter to an editor and another published commentary both of which emphasize our dire need to have our schools adequately staffed with teachers as well as a greater need for our American communities to place emphasis on social education to support the efforts of our battle-weary teachers.

Many things are being cut back on in this country. I suppose we could say our conditions have resulted in the fat (excesses) being cut back. In times like these going back to the basics is wise. Our children are falling by the wayside and our commitment to change will need to address their needs along with our economic affairs.

In the letter entitled, "Tough times? /Drastic Measures!", I attempt to discourage teacher layoffs as I believe our children need all the help they can get. And in the commentary "Overcoming In Spite of Obstacles," I attempt to give a picture of three crucial areas of concern regarding the social development of our youth. In essence it is critical that our society commits to the overall development of our youth and young adults, who by the way are our future.

* * *

Tough Times? / Drastic Measures!

Last week as I read a commentary by the brass at a local School district, I couldn't help but think about the fact that these are tough times which call for drastic measures. They reported and attempted to validate their decision to lay off some of our country's educators. In addition, the St. Louis Public School district is currently proposing several school closings. These issues along with others are particularly disturbing as we see more and more youth fall by the wayside. Our two fold mission as a country seems to be to improve our fledgling economy while we bolster the integrity and morality of our society.

In order to accomplish such objectives unity is essential. I think one key ingredient to achieving the necessary unification for positive change to occur is a commitment to sacrifice. When president elect Barack Obama said we have more work to do on election night, I believe sacrifice was a large part of what he was calling us to supply.

Sacrifice to keep more teachers employed so that we can return to our old ways of success. Our country is only as good as the people and our people are only as good as the education they acquire which results in better performance. It is clear our society must be educated in the areas of wants and needs as well as courtesy and respect. Our commitment to the idea of sacrifice during these tough times is essential. Dismantling our educational system is not the answer under any circumstances.

Some of our traditional educational practices are still effective but because of a new type of student that has developed out of neglect, abuse, exposure to poor habits etc, we need "New jack" educators. Finding ways to assist our current system by adding educational assistance to help students stay in school, get along better with peers, respect authority, be more responsible and transition into their rightful roles as citizens is essential.

Martin Luther King once said that "the function of education, therefore, is to teach one to think intensively and to think critically. But education which stops with efficiency may prove the greatest menace to society. The most dangerous criminal may be a man gifted in reason but with no morals." Today we have some gifted in reason but morality seems to be at an all time low. We must find better ways to engage our students and therefore budget cuts which remove the front line soldiers (teachers) is unacceptable.

Years ago, the education system whetted the appetites of children and they therefore wanted to do something and be somebody. Today we must overcome the obstacles present in the home life of many of our children by providing them with direction (mental health), motivation (vision) and inspiration (love). Cutting staff is not the way. Find the money and find a way to rehire the staff. In order for education to be effective in these tough times we need to take drastic measures to make sure the money is available.

Allif Dove
February 18, 2009

* * *

Overcoming In Spite Of Obstacles

When prayer and an acknowledgment of our country (such as pledging allegiance) were officially removed from school, I who attended public schools in the 1970's and 1980's can say essential attitudes such as courtesy, respect and unity began to deteriorate. Among the many repercussions were the loss of understanding of self and less realization of the need for both conflict resolution skills and the development of coping mechanisms for school aged children.

It may appear that these responsibilities should be fulfilled at home but I submit first, that the home life of our youth, for many reasons, is not what it once was. And second, even years ago when socially acceptable behavior was taught at home it was reinforced in the community, which included interaction at school. A good example of why practicing learned behavior is important is to consider the fact that although a doctor or dentist may go to school, graduate and be certified by their profession, their status as a doctor or dentist is validated as such only when it is reinforced by successful practice on patients. And so, it should be with the development of our children in their schools and in community-based programs, where they spend seven to eight hours and in some cases even more time each day. These institutions and or organizations should be utilized as platforms where socially acceptable behavior is taught and reinforced. This reinforcement regarding core values concerning adequate conduct, involves the observation, oversight and if necessary correction, to enhance these educational experiences for our children. We must play a greater role in this vital issue of conduct and interpersonal development or else our children will grow up to be criminals if they get to grow up at all.

As I conclude, I simply hope to encourage groups who want to help their country to help youth learn to do these three things. One, know yourself, which means accepting that all humans have things they do well and things they don't do well. Work on weakness and learn to use strengths in a positive, productive and progressive way. Two, learn to expect conflict from time to time and find a way to address conflict that results in the least amount of detriment as possible. And three, and probably the most critical, learn to find positive ways to cope with negative emotions.

I'm sure these suggestions may sound like stress management tips and in some ways, they have a likeness. But since our children are developing, they can find positive ways such as drawing, writing, reading and discussing those emotions in lieu of using drugs, over indulging in playing video games and or over eating, including abusive eating, which contributes to health issues both physical and mental. There is no question that as a whole our youth (our future leaders) are headed in the wrong direction, but with programs that truly address these three areas of development, we can redirect their course and enjoy our future as a country.

Allif Dove
November 14, 2010

* * *

VI

6. Courage

cour·age
noun

**The ability to do something that frightens one
and strength in the face of pain or grief.**

Principle: Courage

With less than 10 years of elected service at less than 50 years of age and a skin tone and heritage that was different from past occupants of America's top office, Senator Barack Obama courageously ran for President of the United States of America. He not only ran. He studied, he traveled, he answered questions and he continuously excelled during his run. He clocked in each day on the campaign trail and has continued to do so during his term in office. Our President has been visible and vocal from day one. His leadership has been truly exemplary.

Since taking office in 2009, President Barack Obama has aggressively tackled problem after problem, seemingly with one goal in mind. That goal appears to be the welfare of the United States. And while no man's motives can be exclusively beyond reproach, he has consistently shown his actions support the recovery of America. The President's courage to seek office in the wake of many problems is only matched by his continuously bold message to Americans to work together.

In this chapter on courage, I would like to first share a Poem entitled "Journey", which I believe embodies this historic movement in a critical moment in United States history and captures some of the concerns at that time. This is followed by a short letter entitled "What You Can Do For Your Country" (unpublished). This letter encourages any American concerned about our welfare to join our President in taking a stand to help us to stand.

Currently the world around us is coming to see more each day the detriments of dictatorship and the benefits of democracy. However democracy is highly dependent on a participatory spirit. It must be under-girded by education but not only education but education motivated by a desire to achieve both (equally) a quality society and a successful life. And when it comes to seeking such a society, courage is indispensable.

The type of courage necessary is to consistently be on the

lookout for the greater good for all and what role you might play in achieving that objective. After all, the true design of civilization is that we all need each other. And here in America today our ability to courageously seek solutions that first ensure our recovery, second improve our system and finally solidify the idea of democracy for the world to know it works is of the utmost importance at this time.

Do we have the courage to stand, to stand together and to do, as my good friend P.M. Brown Jr. always says, "Simply do the right thing, because it is the right thing to do."

* * *

Journey

When did your journey start?
We hear one day your road came to a fork.

Where did you come from?
It seems you were born to run.

You set your sights on the unthinkable!
They said your goal was unreachable!

Economy and Industry were very bleak.
Many felt the current leadership was weak.

You gathered some early support.
They were faithful, loyal and refused to abort!

You stood before huge crowds,

And uttered your answers clear and loud.

As you elegantly spoke,
Your words incited hope.

They said it would never work.
Yet you stand before us as the first.

Now as we start this new journey day by day.
We know new leadership has come to stay.

Because the people said, "put an end to this drama"!
And for America's top job, "We choose Mr. Obama!

By Grace of God
Allif Dove
February 8, 2009

* * *

What You Can Do For Your Country

President John F. Kennedy was famous for saying "Ask not what your country can do for you, but what you can do for your country." And if we look at our recent past up to today there is no question our country can use the collective help of each of our citizens. The last ten years in American politics have been very providential to say the least. After eight years of seemingly silent discontentedness, we emerged upon a time when every one made claims about caring for America and having remedies for her recovery. As a result we see that "America the beautiful" has increasingly become a battle ground with much disarray.

We have had problems emerge continuously while our paid officials respond with their usual bickering. Rarely have they sought to compromise where either side said let's agree on something and all do our best to make it work. We know that soldiers take oaths, police officers take oaths and husbands and wives join in holy matrimony. And while we know some of the oaths are broken, we also know many among these groups truly seek to understand and make things work before calling it quits. Our soldiers do it because they care about the safety of our country; the police officers do it to help to maintain order in society and parents for the welfare of the family. But with many of our elected officials the oath to serve their constituency and the union seems to be lost.

Therefore, it seems fitting that a statement like the one made years ago by President John F. Kennedy should be strongly considered. I submit that any individual seeking to preserve America should participate in the government considering the welfare of our country first. Second, those who care could commit to selecting officials that hold a "country first" attitude as evidenced by how they live. And third, but very important, ensure that officials who hold office, but fail to serve our collective best interest, be evicted, terminated or impeached at once. Then we will be doing for our country what is best.

Allif Dove
February 22, 2011
On America, for America

* * *

VII

7. Sacrifice

sac·ri·fice
noun or verb

An act of offering of something precious and of value.

Principle: Sacrifice

One day at work as we discussed the state of America, my boss reminded us that the Roman Empire did not fall as a result of outside forces. He said in effect that inner ills manifested thru selfishness, resulting in corruption, was what had killed an effective and successful government. I suppose many historians can find other reasons why this government was not able to maintain the height it had reached but most professionals who solve problems would generally agree that external problems are difficult to solve when you have internal division. And the 2010 State of the Union address by President Barack Obama was evidence of the divide in America.

The President's call for unity was met by a cold front by most of the GOP. This resistance included Senator John McCain who after defeat in the November 2008 Presidential Election gave a speech which included the idea of working together.

There is clearly a force in the land that continues to instigate indifference by constantly bickering back and forth about the economy, health care, national security, etc. The President is "busting his butt" to work with individuals that focus on money and not on people. He continues to encourage the development of programs for people that are effective in developing well prepared productive citizens. Even when our President encourages children and young adults, which by the way any caring adults would do, he's met with resistance.

In 2010 we heard in the news about a situation in which our President encouraged young people to stay focused on their goals and make sound decisions regarding their money. This advice was met with hostility and in fact a public servant from the state of Nevada went so far as to say the President was not welcomed there. As citizens of the *United States*, we might say to this man "Who are you to say our President is not welcome anywhere in this country?" In fact, what kind of message does this send about the unity of our United States to other countries?

Here's a question for some of those who continue to resist our President's efforts. If a person you loved was trapped in a building that was on fire and only one fireman could get through to get them, would you ask if he were black or white, rich or poor, democrat or republican? That's okay, don't answer.

Are you in resistance to America getting better? Have you allowed words from others to fog the true issues of a recovering land? America is beautiful. Many long to visit. Surely our liberties are a source of pleasure and comfort. As my wife sits across the table eating oatmeal mixed with raisin bran cereal along with toast covered with blueberry yogurt and a big smile on her face, I am acutely aware that someone is just longing for something to eat somewhere near and far. Can a man help another man? Can our government rebound and improve the quality of life of its citizens?

As my wife finished her breakfast she stated out of nowhere, "that the statement, it takes money to make money" should actually be "it takes money to improve your situation" . While I believe I understand the meaning of the first statement, I too like the second better. Surely at this time in America our goal should be to use our resources to improve our lives across the country. These resources include time, money, information, ideas and talents. Our citizens have power and golden opportunity to propel this country to new heights. Let's harness this power and work on one accord for the preservation, acceleration and utilization of this land and governmental system that God has blessed us with.

73

There are many programs in America and surely, we know that these programs are designed to help solve problems. Programs are for problems that people have. These programs are developed, implemented and overseen by people. The clients of these programs are hungering and thirsting for a change and if information, understanding and motivation don't spring from these programs, the problems they are designed to provide support for will at best go unaddressed. I say at best unaddressed because some programs actually make the situation of their client worse when they don't recognize the importance of treating the client with dignity and respect. As I often share with colleagues, we first treat the person and then we can treat the disorder. If a program does not respect the precious life of each of its' participants, I believe it is only a matter of time before it begins to unravel and be ineffective if it does not redirect properly.

I would like to use this opportunity to share two commentaries ("Moved With Compassion" and "The Common Denominator") which I believe echo the true essence of the sacrificial mindset and actions necessary to help others recover from their disorder and subsequently help our society.

* * *

Moved With Compassion

Have you ever been somewhere and it seemed you were not supposed to be there? Then after a while you realized that perhaps it was in fact meant for you to be there? That was my experience on Friday September 18, 2009 at about 3:10 pm when the 69 commencement of the St. Louis City Drug court program was nearing its conclusion. As I sat in Division 16 on the fifth floor of the Mel Carnahan building, I was impressed with the architectural design of the courtroom with its high ceilings and the gravely serious appearance. Earlier as I awaited the start of the ceremony, my mind quickly flashed to the idea for some but the fact for me that one day I'll have this feeling when I stand before my Maker. My anxiety rose even more when I thought of the inventory of my actions that will be judged at that time. It was a quick and crucial thought. Happily, for me that time has not come but with regard to 13 American citizens and residents of the St. Louis metropolitan area, the time has come for an earthly judgment of sorts. Today these men and women had all fulfilled the requirement of a program which by all appearances has provided them with literally a new freedom and countless other benefits.

The session was opened by two men wearing black robes. As they entered, we rose and shortly after they led us as we all pledged allegiance to the United States flag. These two men, Commissioner (Judge) James Sullivan and Commissioner (Judge) Michael Noble, were made known to anyone who didn't know who they were. The first item on the agenda was to reunite a woman and her children. As a result of fulfilling the Drug court program successfully, she was officially awarded custody of her five children by an official from the Missouri Division of Family Services. This emotional and inspirational moment was intensified as the family embraced and everyone else cheered and clapped. This event was immediately followed by another reunification when another young lady, whose child was taken at birth, was literally handed back her baby as a result of successfully completing the program and maintaining 13 continuous months of sobriety. These truly touching cases of redemption were no doubt initiated by people having compassion for individuals in need.

As both Commissioner Sullivan and Commissioner Noble presided over this truly meaningful event in our society, they took turns reading commentaries on each graduate that told about their journey through the program. These commentaries were colorfully prepared by their diversion managers. Men and women who tirelessly helped these clients navigate their lives back into manageability by ensuring they understood and adhered to the guidelines of this sound program. Listening carefully, I heard (between the lines) the building of character and dedication. I heard how individuals who once lacked accountability and responsibility had now come to recognize, respect, appreciate and embody these qualities.

Following these heartfelt commentaries, a representative from the St. Louis City Prosecutor's office came forth and read an official letter, dismissing the very charges that brought the graduates into the program. She then joined both commissioners as all the graduates' received certificates and letters as appropriate. While I was not a recipient, I imagined the sigh of relief the graduates must have felt since many were facing long prison sentences if they did not complete the program. An opportunity made possible only through care, compassion and dedicated workers.

The next phase of this commencement allowed us to hear directly from the graduates. This is unique because usually at ceremonies such as these, the graduates receive a motivational speech. But being the educational experience that the Drug court seems to have developed into, Commissioner Sullivan advised each graduate that they were now successful products of a program committed to restoring lives and benefiting communities. He advised them that they were now "a part of the solution" of helping others to do exactly what was done for them.

As each graduate, who chose to, rose and spoke, they expressed gratitude for the opportunity to participate in the program, gave special thanks to the commissioners and the other committed professionals that helped them and gave words of encouragement as well as warnings to many other current Drug court participants who were sitting in the audience. Hearing stories about these positive outcomes which involved progress such as restored families, graduations, gaining employment, starting a business and returning to school, I could not help but appreciate the opportunity they had received to restore their lives and the gift of hope and encouragement they were now able to pass on. All of which is due to the caring and collectively good actions of people along with the good management of a good program.

And as for me, I wound up at this affair when I called an old friend whom I have had the privilege of working with in an unofficial capacity, through his journey to stay sober and build a better life. The call was made a few days earlier when he informed me of his graduation. Always enthused by a good outcome or happy ending, I instantly stated I planned to attend. To make certain that I would be there, out of nowhere my boss gave me that entire day off (I usually work a half day on Fridays). At the graduation and while seated in the courtroom, Commissioner Sullivan asked all professionals who work with individuals in treatment and in recovery from addictions to stand. Although I had not been working with these drug court participants in an official capacity, I too stood among those professionals asked to stand and I happily did so.

And finally, as I thought about the things I had read about Jesus Christ, what I remembered most was that sometimes when Jesus fed and healed people in need the Bible tells us He was moved with compassion or that he loved those that He was feeding or healing. That is the same feeling I felt when I observed the activities in Division 16. It was apparent that although both judges and the many helpful professionals had positions of power and authority, they were no doubt moved with compassion as evidenced by the way these individuals have been helped in the process of rebuilding their lives.

One other note that I failed to mention was that Judge Sullivan acknowledged and thanked a Missouri State Representative in attendance, whose name I don't know. But the point being that this program works and if it and others like it are to continue to work, funding must be available. Politicians like this one, who took the time to attend such a worthy event, can see for themselves the fruit of a successful program by attending these commencements.

The St. Louis City Drug Court program works! Especially when loving, caring, competent and compassionate people, like this host of people, are moved to get together and work together to help the needy. By the way, now I am sure I was meant to be there, because my confidence in this effective program and others like it, has grown a little more.

Allif Dove
November 19, 2009

* * *

We The People... Our Common Denominator

In recent news in the St. Louis area two stories that really caught my attention were on involving the public request that the case involving Reginald Clemons be reconsidered and the other was a case in which a respectable police Lieutenant across the river in Illinois was senselessly murdered but very heroically the people of the community pulled together to solve his murder. Although these cases were contrasting, they both involved a person raising a question, other people getting involved and things changing for good because of a common denominator is the collective, caring and consistent action for the people. These actions proved once again that "Yes we can". However, in another national story this common denominator "We the people" seemed to be sadly missing.

In both of these cases, people went above and beyond the call of duty. This is true dedication (love and concern) for our society, which at times has been very sick. We need sacrifices such as these to investigate and find the right verdict but also to train our youth as well as those who are misguided, uninformed or unskilled at overcoming obstacles. This practice of utilizing our valuable common denominator "We the people" was apparently missing and absent in another man's life, which seemed to contribute to a fatal ending. The death of Michael Jackson was both unexpected and tragic and has received major attention. And although we can't do much, if anything, for Michael Jackson there is certainly something we can learn from his death.

An age-old question from the Bible is "Am I my brother's keeper?" (Gen 4:9). And if we think about Mr. Jackson and all of his humanitarian efforts including making music committed to encouraging love and brotherhood as well as his very liberal giving of both self and money, one could certainly say he acted as in the "brother's keeper" concept. Yet, on the other hand, did we miss his cry for understanding, compassion and support. Changes in his physical features, the obvious pain from some of his life experiences, such as physical pain associated with performing and frustration with business and legal issues, could have worn him down physically, emotionally, mentally and spiritually. Did "We the people" love the performer but look past his human frailties? As he sang, "They don't really care about us," I wonder "We the people," who loved his music, were the "they" that failed to really care about him. *(So many of our American performers suffer and need support as well.)*

Michael Jackson once sang the lyrics to a song with Rockwell stating "I always feel like somebody's watching me." Well, someone is watching us and most of us call that someone God. And I think God wants us to look out for each other. Michael, along with many other stars proclaimed "We are the world" and that "we've got to make this world a better place, so let's start giving.' And while he left a rich legacy of humanitarian lyrics to encourage us to help others, it also seems obvious that many of us enjoyed him especially for his excellence, energy and creativity, but because of his success and monetary riches, we all may have missed his plea for help. So, let's appreciate Michal Jackson, and other great artist, for their humanitarian spirit, which after all is God given and then try to begin to "look over our shoulders" for the next struggling soul, remembering that it doesn't matter "if they are black or white" because "we've "got to be there" for each other. And PS: I'm also "talking to the man in the mirror."

Allif Dove
July 13, 2009

* * *

82

VIII

8. Accountability

ac·count·a·bil·i·ty

noun

The acknowledgment of and assumption of responsibility for actions, products, decisions, and policies.

Principle: Accountability

Before I wrote this chapter I asked a few people what they felt this word meant. Surprisingly the answers I received basically boiled down to I don't know. One friend however did go and look the word up and later during a conversation about my procrastination in finishing this book he told me that the word accountability meant liability. Or in other words an accountable person would be seen as one who could be liable or *answerable for something.*

In today's society our news is filled with innuendos, accusations and outright questions about how to account for what is happening. Who's the blame, what's the answer, how can it be fixed, what should be done, what step should we take next? Where does true blame lie or better yet what is the solution?

As I reflect on my earliest remembrance in life regarding life and the quality of, I quickly became aware of words like economy, inflation, the government, politicians and taxes. I would also hear about racism and its' believed role in our American society. These two culprits (government and racism) became the scapegoats, the answerable ones for the tragedy that our citizens experienced whether it is marked by a loss of jobs, high gas prices or an overall lack of a quality life.

My continued growth, exposure and education brought about new ideas about where the answers to problems such as those most citizens are concerned with should come from. Let's face it everyone wants to be happy and therefore wants solutions, but where, from who and how shall it come? Many people have lost hope and wonder when and, in some minds, if change will come.

Can this great nation, with such a strong history of success, with a pronounced belief in God and a concept of being united find the answer necessary to insure its welfare and health. We are in a survival mode and certainly need to clarify this question of answerability. Who shall be held liable for our rise or fall, for our victory or defeat? Whose job is it to be accountable, answerable and liable? Is it the U.S. president, is it the U.S. congress or is it the education system. Is it God or is it the people who express their belief in God. The question is where does the logical obligation lie?

In my search for clarity regarding this word, I found that it closely paralleled the word responsibility, yet there is a difference. The difference appears to me to be that accountability refers to the obligation to commit to something while the responsibility has to do with the overall requirement for the outcome of something.

With regard to the obligation to commit to something it seems logical that every concerned citizen would be more than willing to develop a better quality of life in a country many of us have had pleasant experiences in. It stands to reason that in the same manner our citizens fought in the revolutionary war that our citizens today would be just as willing to wage war on our poor performance as a country. Yes, I did say poor performance because we must be truly honest about where we are in order to move to where we would like to be.

I'm sure by now you know what I am about to say. Yes, it is not the governments' fault, it is not the politicians' fault and it's not the education systems fault! It is our fault! We are responsible as citizens to develop into accountable citizens. In other words, we must hold ourselves accountable. There are many reasons why we have fallen into seriously troubled waters and the most basic of these reasons is always one common variable and that is the American citizen. We must ask ourselves if we have loved the pleasures but not invested enough in the success of this country. And I believe there are three primary areas of concern for each citizen to consider if we are to work towards the formation of a more perfect nation.

In this chapter I will use a poem ("Fix This Mess") and two letters ("Our True State" and "Digging Deep") to highlight the importance of self education and realization, the benefits of developing spiritually and the necessity to pass on the idea of purposing to become a well-developed citizen who is committed to making an impact for a better society.

* * *

Fix This Mess

Answer big, answer loud!
And answer as often as needed.
See what's wrong with our babies!
See what's required to rescue them.
No clue about life.
Filled with hurt,
Acknowledged thru anger and
Frustrated by ignorance.
Ignorance from adults, who know their state,
Yet fail to unify, commit and seek God's grace.
God will answer, direct and protect.
And if we obey, He will teach us to fix this mess.

* * *

Our True State

Since President Obama's State of the Union address in January, much has been written about the country. I purposely chose to use the word country rather than union because since the signing of the stimulus package, we have been everything but a union. In fact, most if not all leaders in the Republican Party, have publicly voiced opposition to decisions made concerning our government. These decisions, by the way, were made using our democratic process. These leaders have yet to utter a word about unity or taking the decisions that were made and making the best of them.

Many times we have heard why things can't work instead of how we can make them work together. Let's remember a little less than ten years ago when George W. Bush was narrowly declared the winner in a questionable Presidential election over Al Gore. And although many were frustrated and some outraged, the rest of the country including Democrats pulled together to work to have the best union we could. In fact, even as our former president continued to make poor decisions, the union still stuck together. I wonder why some individuals like Sarah Palin, Dick Cheney and Newt Gingrich could not be heard in opposition during a time of gross mismanagement but nevertheless now are so vocal when our country should be on the mend.

Even worse today is the lack of respect these Republican leaders have for our government and laws. Our president and other elected officials have been repeatedly disrespected and harassed for excising their proper delegated authority as elected officials. If we are committed to democracy, as we have always been, it is up to us to recognize when the rights under our system are being violated or manipulated and promptly address that matter.

As Duke University won yet another NCAA Division 1 title it gives us all a reminder of the importance of good leadership and a good system of rules. Coach Mike Krzyzewski undoubtedly has a good strategy for success but as with all good teams, organizations or countries it still takes people working that system together. Unity is an indispensible key to success and our country must find our way back and this begins with good leadership.

No one can threaten, intimidate or harass a public servant (regardless of their party) because if we allow such actions to go on, we are no longer functioning as a democracy. If we do not defend this critical portion of our standards in the United

States of America, we will have journeyed from a Union into a state of emergency which will most likely be followed by total chaos.

Allif Dove
April 5, 2010

* * *

Digging Deep

As I listened to some of the Republican candidates this past week as they geared up for their Presidential run, one word rang loud in my ear and it was "Rhetoric!" There is always one way to spot a weak or insecure candidate and that is they will focus more on the other guy. During the numerous speeches made, if we heard Obama once it's highly possible we heard his name hundreds of times as candidate after candidate used this angle to secure leverage. However, after all of the rhetoric is released and the candidate has to reveal some truths about themselves, here is where we the American people must focus on what is right, good and profitable.

Here is a good example why all information should be examined. The GOP candidates including those of the tea party will tell us point blank "Obama bailed out big business." In fact, however, we should consider if big business went unchecked for 8 years (under Bush Administration 01-08) racking up enormous debt, exploiting workers and driving companies into the ground. We should remember that Chief Executive Officers, hired to steer companies through turbulence and to success, literally took the money leaving employees high and dry. Then considering the economic damage caused by such actions, we should ask if the bailouts were necessary. Were they necessary to keep companies, with pension responsibilities and thousands of employees in limbo, afloat? But if we simply hear the rhetoric and fail to dig deeper, we will be seduced into electing someone who won't have a country first attitude.

And although President Obama may not be, in the eyes of some, the most patriotic president in history he has nevertheless, time after time, spoken and acted with a country first attitude. We should keep in mind that what's best for the country may not always be popular. Thus with this in mind, we as fellow Americans should dig deep because the 2012 election results will determine if we as citizens are committed to thoroughly sifting through rhetoric and finding the best candidate for America's top job.

Allif Dove
June 20, 2011

* * *

IX

9. Responsibility

re·spon·si·bil·i·ty
noun

**The state or fact of having a duty to deal with
something or of having control over someone.**

Principle: Responsibility

When I wrote the commentary, "This Is It!", there seemed to be a vast number of irresponsible acts by many highly visible citizens. And although these acts negatively impacted our society these individuals could have positively impacted our society by simply acting in a more responsible way. To act in a responsible manner means to talk the talk and walk the walk that contributes to reconstruction and production in our society and not the destruction of it. In addition to the commentary "This Is It!", I also included in this chapter are a commentary ("Responsible To Ensure Accountability") and two letters ("Once Again America" and "Hoodwinked Again"). All of these writings embody the idea that each American citizen is responsible to make their abilities available, their voice heard, their action felt and their votes count because during this time of recovery our collective and best efforts are drastically needed.

* * *

This Is It!

In so much as today is envisioned to be "A New Day" of sorts, since America chose a platform of change and solidified it with the election of our country's first African-American president, let us reflect on the progress to date. Although much of what we accomplish these days is gagged by scientific evidence, surveys, polls and the like, of greater significance is the social barometer of the society in which we live. A quick scan of recent events reveals the harshness of our community and the sporadic conduct that has been oozing out over our landscape. Surely so many insensitive acts are not indicative of the values we foreshadow for the world to see. But the hardcore reality of the matter is what's in you is going to come out of you.

In recent events, a U.S. Senator serving in one of our country's most important leadership positions, a well-known tennis pro, an entertainer at an awards gala and a group of stars including film makers all say and do things contradictory to what we believe to be the American way. Sure, there is freedom of speech but this was not meant to overshadow courtesy, respect and appreciation for the personhood of others and not to mention our responsibility of teaching our children the proper way to do things by example. And although we have experienced progress with regard to our economy and our health care system, there is an "issue" that is largely responsible for the state we are currently in and desperately need to work out of. Yes, that "issue" or "attitude" that if we fail to attend to it; it will cause us to remain in the condition we are currently attempting to work through.

This attitude of *me, myself and I and forget everybody else.* That quiet deep inner self that says this is my life, my future and my career while at the same time utilizing the help of family, employers and educational institutions to achieve goals. That attitude hinders one's ability to realize that in reality there is no way one can achieve ultimate goals like happiness and success alone, and that such an attitude also keeps one from recognizing the importance of unity. It prohibits the understanding of how beginning and maintaining the practice of encouraging, inspiring and rooting for each other is a critical step towards making a real and lasting change. Such a change in individual attitudes would effectively put the old way of doing business out of the window. Michael Jackson, Lionel Richie and friends proclaimed this belief like this "We are the world, we are the future... so let's start giving."

So much of what we read today focuses on the problems we have. Sure, we are in recovery but recovery is not simply about a single issue such as economics or health care, it is about the attitude and actions that led to the downfall. On an individual level it is conceivable that a poor financial decision can lead to a setback. But thinking about our condition on a national level, one might ask if recessions and depressions are the result of long-lasting policies that don't work?

One thing about recovery, if it is to be successful, is that when you begin to address change, there must be an understanding that everything about your operating procedures comes under review and is subject to revision. Old mindsets and strategies must be closely scrutinized and abandoned if they prove unproductive. America did not achieve its' highest level of living simply by what we said but it was by what was done and the same can be said about our current status. Quite frankly we must ask if we have promoted the liberation available here while slipping on the need to exercise the wisdom and discretion that is necessary to insure these liberties. Two areas in which this question must be answered are regarding our public information channels and another is the service rendered by our elected officials.

A good example of how information can be effective is when we were told that the way we access public television (analog) would change. Prior to the effective date there was support to get the information out as well as support on how to prepare and be ready for the change. As we go thru this change regarding one of the most serious times in American history, let us understand what singer Kenny Loggins said when he sang "This is it, make no mistakes where you are, you are going no further." It would be foolish to presume that we can succeed in this critical stage of our history without turning over every stone and offering the best collective solutions to each pothole we find. Our media must lead the way in this charge and the responsibility must be rooted in "United we stand and divided we fall." Can we stand to write about and report on solutions while avoiding bickering and finger pointing? We must remember, "This is it."

Of equal importance is the service we receive from the local, state and federal executives that we pay. Our elected representatives, who draft the bills that become our laws, should be held to a standard of true service primarily because it is our very lives and futures that are on the line. Each constituent that is capable must keep an eye on the overall performance of their elected official to include how they vote and why they voted that way, for we must remember "This is it." Why, you may ask, do I say, "This is it?" To that, I say, if we keep doing what we have done then we will keep getting what we have gotten. And if we do that, we are in serious trouble! Now is the time for serious change. This change is centered in our attitude and can be best filtered out through a caring and informed media and by elected officials that are sensitive to the needs of the people while acting in the best interest of our beloved nation. Remember; This…is… it!

* * *

Responsible To Ensure Accountability

n my opinion I believe anyone speaking about the Trayvon Martin story should first sincerely offer condolences to his family. Therefore "To the family of this precious young man, I pray that God eases your pain, comforts your heart and allows the memory of Trayvon to inspire us all to live life to the fullest and to good purpose."

Based on how he lived, Trayvon was obviously a very decent and good young man. For that reason alone, I subscribe to what his father said at a rally, when he said, "Trayvon did not deserve to die." Yet we will all die someday, unless Jesus returns first, but young Trayvon did not deserve to die in this manner. Therefore, since he did not deserve to die in this way, what is our proper response? Seeking justice is the prevailing thought and rightfully so.

We all know that racial profiling motivated by hate, fear, indifference, guilt, pride, selfishness, greed and many other negative sources, is a common and everyday occurrence in America. Thus, in reality we may never fully know the mindset of Mr. Zimmerman (the man who shot Trayvon). What we do know for sure is he put his thoughts into action at that moment resulting in young Trayvon's death. I ask myself at this very moment why was Trayvon not rushed to the hospital or miraculously found alive in the morgue? For some reason, Trayvon was not saved and not allowed to continue this life, but why?

This reminds me of the many unjust acts that have stemmed from poor thoughts and resulted in detrimental outcomes. Jesus died for the sins of the world, Dr. Martin Luther King Jr. died for justice, President Abraham Lincoln died for emancipation, President John F. Kennedy died for fairness and Malcolm X died for truth. The common denominator of all of these incidents is accountability. Just as these men sought accountability, we are responsible to stand up for right… *no matter what!* Could the death of young Trayvon (if you can accept this idea) be a sacrifice to cause us to seek and insist on accountability?

No human being can *force* anyone to think or believe anything. However, if an individual should think a negative thought, then commit a negative act and as a result hurt someone wrongfully, *we the people* have a *responsibility* as a citizen to ensure that this individual is held accountable for their actions. Therefore, *we the people* are right to seek the truth and insist that a just retribution be paid for this precious life that was lost.

Recently I heard someone on television discussing the case of young Trayvon and putting the focus on the hoodie worn by Trayvon. I quickly thought to myself "Don't get it twisted!" This issue is not about clothes, hate, profiling, and racism or about prejudice. While I understand many of these sources do usually lead to bad acts such as hate crimes, I believe our focus in this case, at this time and in this season should be on our responsibility to seek accountability. And the actual method to accomplish this is Love. Yes Love, because Love will make you do right, treat others right, and help you develop courage to change. Will we allow Love to motivate us to seek justice in Trayvon's case? And if we do, then the life of young Trayvon will have been sacrificed to bring about more harmony. So let's hold those needing it accountable for their actions. We are responsible to seek to build a better society. Remember Jesus is Love and his Love will help us do right.

Allif Dove
March 24, 2012

* * *

Once Again America

Nearly two years ago America experienced a life changing event, that being the election of America's first African-American president. Since then discontent to say the least has been ever so present. Whether calling President Barack Obama an alien or a Muslim he has been labeled anything but America's president. This attitude, of course, is well within any citizen's right considering the many liberties we enjoy including freedom of speech. But although we have this liberty, let's not forget the fact that freedom of choice comes at a price.

That price is duty. It is the relentless performance of many Americans and surely God's favor that allows us to stand even in an unstable economy. So, as we move towards the next presidential election let us remember two years ago we took a stand for change. Our president has made decisions that in essence invest in the lives of America's people. He has acted with the knowledge that if business and government are to assume and maintain their rightful positions in the life of America, that this is better achieved when each American is healthy, hopeful, educated and wholly committed to contributing to the American Dream.

So once again America, yes, we can, if we again remember the stand we as a country have taken. Yes, we can if we acknowledge that change involves recognizing error, stopping that direction, redirecting, practicing a new way and staying committed to that way. Yes, we can, if we realize that under President Obama and the current administration we are functioning in a positive process of change. And yes, we can, if as a country, we refuse to be tricked out of our earned progress that will get better and better if we work for it.

Allif Dove
October 10, 2010

* * *

Hoodwinked Again

Recently a well-known New York politician was found to be indulging in inappropriate sexual escapades via the World Wide Web. This was especially troubling to many American citizens because of the serious state of affairs we face.

These affairs, of serious nature, being our economy and foreign affairs, are daily and sometimes hourly reported on. And while these are important, the essence of our ability to succeed in these areas is a matter of character.

Not like a character on television but the very character of a wise man. This is obviously what the U.S. Congressman lacks. And although the news is currently about his treatment and plans to return to his duties in public office, it should be about why we as citizens fail to spot imposters that have no intention of putting the duties of their office first.

Yes America, as you get prepared for election 2012, ponder this question. Why do we continue to get had, hoodwinked and bamboozled into wasting our money on fellow citizens who won't put "We the people" first? Please tell me why?

Allif Dove
June 14, 2011

* * *

X

10. Support

sup·port
verb

Bear all or part of the weight of; hold up.

Principle: Support

In America, we are in dire need of education. This statement might prompt one to say why would you say a country that has a good education system needs education. Well to that I would say, not a traditional education but an education that requires us to learn the value of seeking to live in harmony. This country has a good system for the education of its citizens, but based on the number of violent incidents and constant social turmoil it is reasonable to deduce that the education related to character is at least somewhat lacking. Conversely, looking to the extreme, it could be argued that the quality of our education is significantly insufficient as it has to do with character building. Thus, when one is taught more about achieving with little or no emphasis placed on how to achieve and how to enjoy their achievements there is a strong chance that decent values will be overlooked.

The idea of living according to principles that contribute to the idea of freedom and liberty for all must be instilled as it was in years past if we are to successfully overcome our present-day situation. Any modern-day Politician that does not see the state of emergency we are in with regard to education is most likely one who should be ignored like a plague. In this chapter I provide two poems ("What Am I?" and "Pass It Down") along with one short story ("Momma Tell Me The Truth") and two serious commentary to ("Restoration & Recovery, A Message To Remember") to help to emphasis the dire need for support of one another if we are to be truly successful as a country.

As we explore the idea of social education, I simply encourage the capitalist to consider this idea. Although it is a good idea to be able to go from rags to riches and from poverty to prosperity, I submit to you that the way it is done and the way it is kept has a supreme bearing on the society at large. If getting to the top is the most important thing without regard to how one's character affects society as a whole, we have fostered an atmosphere that will most likely wax colder and colder and ultimately result in our demise. As you read this chapter, I hope this idea of supporting one another, as our American Olympians seem to do very well at the games, becomes an embedded pillar to support our efforts to hold up the American standard that declares "United we stand and divided we fall."

* * *

What Am I?

Everything you have ever done originated with me. I was there when you took your first step and when you said Momma for the first time. In fact, everything anybody ever did, both good and bad began with me. I was there when the first house was built and the first house was torn down. I was there when you decided on your first girlfriend or boyfriend. I'm there when men say yes or women say no and vice versa. I'm important, I'm precious and I can lead to wonderful things happening, I'm silly, I'm worthless and I can lead to destruction. Use me right and I will lead you to success. Use me wrong and you'll stay depressed. I pop in and I pop out. When I get you alone, I may be able to kill you but when you share me, I lose my ability to dominate you. Yes I can be powerful and I can move like the wind. I'm everywhere, all the time, involved in everything. I am a thought and the safest place for me when I come to you is to be turned over to God.

So when I come to you; Think, then re-think and think again about me. Talk to someone else about me. Pray about me. And in doing so you will expose me and you will know if I am good or bad, right or wrong, profitable or worthless.

Allif Dove
January 26, 2008

* * *

Pass It Down

To all those who are renowned.
Whose mouth's yield words that are profound.
Your work in motion renders a sweet sound.
As your zest, fervor and success continue to abound.

I saw a boy; he had no food.
Then I saw a girl forcefully throw up in a stool.
Our children are hurt, from treatment so cruel.
They need our help, with living school.

Renowned you say?
Profound you speak?
It's all just a waste,
Unless you abound and teach!

PASS IT DOWN

* * *

Momma Tell Me The Truth

Good morning, Momma. How are you today? I woke up this morning and I know I am blessed. But something happened to me this morning. I felt a strong desire to know about my daddy. Yes I know you say he doesn't care anything about me. I know he won't (or can't) pay child support. I know he left you for that other woman (or the streets). I know you can't stand him. But what I want to know is the truth. Momma told me the truth, the whole truth and nothing but the truth.

Momma I know you love me. I know you have sacrificed for me. I know your struggles. But Momma I also know I am a little older now and I heard the preacher say "the truth will make you free." (John 8:32). Momma I believe that, so I want to know what you thought about when you met my daddy. I want to know what you saw in him. I want to know what were your hopes and dreams. I want to know if he did some things well.

I want to know if he has any gifts or was he special in some way. Do you know what happened to him? Momma told me what happened to him. Momma, can't you see the more I know about my daddy, good and bad, the more I'll know myself and the more I will understand about my character. Why do you dislike him so much? Why does he dislike you so much?

Momma I heard there is this old saying that teaches "It takes a village to raise a child" and when I think about it, my most important people in the village can't stand each other. I heard the preacher say that God commands me to "honor your father and mother, that my days upon the land may be long (Ex 20:12) but because you two dishonor each other with words and actions, I don't know how to truly feel about you both sometimes. I respect you both as my parents but you suck as role models on how to make peace. God said the peace makers would be blessed (Matt 5:9) and I hear you both say God this and God that, but I see you do something different. Someone told me that a man named Rodney King was famous for saying "Can't we all just get along" and I don't know him but I can sure feel him.

Well Momma, I have said a lot, and I mean no disrespect, but I need love. I need it from you and my daddy. I have learned in my short life that God forgives and heals. I know that "All have sinned and come short of the glory of God." (Rom 6:23) So Momma if you don't want me to seek love elsewhere, tell me the truth about God in your words and in your actions because I don't care what my daddy did, I still love him! I love him! And I'm going to write him a letter next week and send it to the prison telling him the same thing about you. And Momma you know why? I am going to do it because God, grandma and the preacher told me that love heals. And I know God is Love because he sent Jesus Christ, His only begotten son, into the world to die for our sins and the more I get to know Jesus, the more freedom I get and the more truth I know and live.

Allif Dove
December 17, 2010

* * *

Recovery & Restoration

Do you remember this song "I believe the children are our future...?" Remember how it was played or sang at a youth event such as a graduation. Remember how everyone would smile or cry when all the little precious, adorable sons, daughters, nieces, nephews or grandchildren would strut across the stage. Oh, how good it felt to think we were getting these children ready to excel. But then the program was over and as we filed out of the assembly we tried to hang on to the idea of making an impact for our future by investing in the lives of these young ones but within a week it was business as usual for most of us. Back to the grind which usually meant less focus on children and more on finances, bills, careers and success. We all can agree that investing in our youth is critical but how can we stay focused on them and the things necessary to take care of them also?

I applaud the efforts of President Barack Obama. It appears that his desire to help young people grasp the idea of developing a hunger and thirst for striving for excellence is genuine. His ability to articulate points and his personal adventure of overcoming odds makes him both a valuable spokesman and a valid/justifiable authority on empowerment. However, we still must realize what we are dealing with, how these things have developed and what keeps us in that state today. In short, what's the cancer and where is it at?

Back in the 1980's as I sat and watched the trial of LTC Oliver North and others on television (regarding the Iran contra affairs), I didn't fully grasp the impact that the core of those discussions would have on our future. Over 25 years later graveyards and prisons are filled. Psychotropic medication sales along with disability claims are at record levels. Retirements and plans for the future for many were destroyed along with property lost and savings annihilated. And last but not least our children are dislocated, neglected, abused, and malnourished (mentally) and are now killing each other.

The state of affairs we are in today has left us with two primary dilemmas. Restoring and or solidifying resources necessary for daily living and reclaiming our youth. And although it seems that these two objectives should be achievable individually it appears they must be worked out collectively. To put it simple we must invest in restoring families which will restore communities and so on. And upon working to restore these families let's remember love and acceptance equals hope. Regardless how bad a person has fallen if they feel genuine forgiveness and acceptance then they develop new hope. Many have fallen into prison, serious mental illness, addiction and other poor lifestyle choices but our ability to overcome these ills are wrapped up in our ability to love. Not to be taken advantage of but to help when needed and when we are able to, recognizing the overall need for love and its true healing power.

Stevie Wonder said it like this: "These three words, short and simple." So as you go about your affairs today, call a relative or a friend and tell them you are willing to help them if they want help but most of all tell them "I love you." Another song writer once expressed the need for this very powerful tool by writing "What the world needs now is love, sweet love; it's the only thing that there is just too little of..." If we, as a country, are to recover, it's going to take sacrifice and lots of love.

Allif Dove
November 14, 2009

* * *

XI

11. Unity

u·ni·ty
noun

The state of being united or joined as a whole.

Principle: Unity

Twisting Words

While getting prepared to go to church services on Mother's Day, I tuned into a weekly nationally televised news show. I listened with high volume ears when I heard the name President Obama. I began to hope that a good report would come forth. My hope today is fueled by the realization that more than ever this country (in critical times) needs both a successful president and a successful government. And it is highly questionable that one can exist without the other. As I focused even more intently on the television, I vaguely recognized an old familiar face. It was former House of Representatives chairman Newt Gingrich. I say vaguely recognized because I am not a close follower of political affairs at all times. But as I listened, I was initially pleased to hear what I felt to be less political rhetoric than in time past. Then I began to listen closer and he lowered the boom!

A question was asked regarding having more or less government and the news show featured some comments from some other politicians.

One statement came from former Secretary of State Colin Powell. General Powell had said in effect "American citizens want more government." When Mr. Gingrich was asked to respond to this he said in effect if you ask American's if they want to pay more taxes, they won't be in favor of doing so. After his reply I began to be reminded of the intense rivalry between the GOP and the Democrats. Does the GOP want less government and the Democrats more government? One fact is certainly etched in history and that is on November 4, 2008 our country functioned with an acute awareness of the seriousness of the state of the union at that time. Our state was and still is worthy of our full attention. This state developed over years and our ability to work through this state will take collective, committed and consistent action. The old rivalries and wars must cease for the best interest of us all.

All of us who truly recognize our state and sincerely desire progress and restoration in this country will understand General Powell's statement. His statement centered around the idea that as President Obama once said "we are not a bunch of Red States or Blue States but we are the United States." What that means to me is that government helps bring us all together. It is designed to work for our use. It works for our protection, direction and our overall betterment. We are to utilize it as we need it but, as we gain better sense of both our collective and individual responsibilities, less of it is needed. But when serious problems exist, this tool (government) is needed to investigate, correlate and regulate our affairs for the survival and subsequent empowerment of us all. Therefore Mr. Gingrich what I think General Powell meant is Americans are willing to pay for more government if it will improve our society and improve the quality of our lives. So in the words of singer Al Green "Let's stay together" or as Rodney King said (even after being beaten) "can we all just get along?"

Allif Dove
May 10, 2009

I expounded on these ideas in more detail with an essay written several years ago entitled "Executing Our Unity."

* * *

Executing Our Unity

Many times, in our society we will hear the word unity used. Usually in times of frustration, chaos and crisis, someone will give a speech or write an article about this essential attribute of success. Yes, this quality can be found in every successful team, organization, company or community. It is not only absolutely, positively necessary, it is indispensable. So, since it is certain we cannot do without it, why is it so illusive when it is most needed? Or in some situations when it can be harnessed, why can't it be sustained? By now you're probably wondering what this article is all about or perhaps you don't feel like wondering so I will just say it's the most critical issue in our society today. It is the issue in our American society.

Let's face it! We have never, in such a short period of time, had so much bad news at the level of high institutions and organizations in our country's history. Sure, there were probably periods in our history when serious issues arose, yet one could argue that those came during times when our society was growing up and dealing with the pains of doing so. But let's also face the fact that, in spite of our advanced education, understanding, technology and systems, we have experienced negative blow after blow in 2008, serious indifference in 2009, more frustration in 2010 and a fierce stalemate like presence in 2011. And although we have experienced continuous hardship during these times, we are still standing and the ball is in our court, allowing us an opportunity to stay banded together so we can emerge victoriously.

Banding together is what we do and thankfully the ideas expressed in the early literature of our government, provides us with a treasure trove of rich concepts that if relentlessly applied, can help us maintain and in the long term, sustain our precious and beloved society. Here are a few that come to mind instantly. "United we stand and divided we fall", "Life, liberty and the pursuit of happiness" and "In God we trust." And what's even more fascinating is how over the years, as well as now, they remain so prevalent if only applied appropriately.

One of our country's founding principles is "United we stand and divided we fall." I find that the motivation to interpret and implement this idea comes better by first grasping the latter half of this phrase (divided we fall). To avoid falling is our objective because we like standing. This country stands so tall in the world, in spite of our deficiencies and what we hear about those who hate our country.

Just think of the feelings you get when you imagine Michael

Phelps standing with the national anthem playing while wearing (count them) eight gold medals or what about Carl Lewis taking a victory lap or our whole Olympic team, dressed in red, white and blue, marching in on opening day. It's that feeling we get when we proudly stand tall and march tall. What about our brave soldiers or the firefighters, policemen and numerous volunteers in New York (and other communities struck by disaster) who stood for those in need. Yes, we find, when we stand together and refuse to "fall" that's when we really stand "tall."

And when difficult times come, we stand tallest when we don't harp on how we got there, so much as on how we will positively move forward from there. Reviewing what has happened and avoiding similar acts is essential to making progressive change, but anything more than that will distract our efforts as we strive to stand.

Another quote from our rich constitution literature is "Life, Liberty and the Pursuit of Happiness." One could say in this country there has been injustice which nevertheless paved the way for change. This change has come at huge prices especially when we think of the deaths of Abraham Lincoln, Malcolm X, Martin Luther King Jr. and John F. Kennedy. Surely, we wouldn't be where we are today without these and many more brave sacrifices from, yes, our own citizens. In fact, such ultimate sacrifices for Life, Liberty and the Pursuit of Happiness are the essence of all monumental change in this country.

When we all consider some of the liberties we have such as shelter, food and clothing along with entertainment, transportation and education, we should be quick to realize we are much more fortunate than most societies in the world. More importantly, we have an opportunity to build on these to gain more for all by committing to sacrifice more for all. Our collective investment in this idea for the improvement of our country actually adds another strong cord to our unity.

Still another cord that binds our unity can be seen on our currency. Yes, somebody once said "Put your money where your mouth is." When we look at our money, we see the words "In God We Trust." Instantly what comes to mind is the person that says "I don't believe in God" or "Keep God out of this", but the fact of the matter is, when we decided to pray to God and acknowledge Him by putting "In God We Trust" on our currency, we put God in it. A common saying in today's society is "If something is not broken don't fix it." It must be working because in spite of the stock market failures, the Great Depression of the 30's, inflation, recessions, unemployment, deficits, wars, and any other financial misfortune we can recall, we are still standing. We are still standing in spite of our decisions and efforts.

So, God must be working on our behalf and since it seems he is working on our behalf, those of us who do trust, should trust and pray for his continued care, protection and guidance. I suppose the ultimate evidence of our trust as a country would be to acknowledge His ways and seek guidance to come into agreement with them. Surely God does not want our women, our young, our disabled and our elderly mistreated, neglected or abused. Surely, He wouldn't see addictions, mutilations and perversions as beneficial to anyone. So maybe prayer for one another and care towards one another can keep us unified. Ronald Reagan, I believe, once called for a "kinder, gentler nation" and in light of our favor from God, total trust in God, as a guiding light in this direction, would be wise.

In conclusion, what comes to mind is a Bible verse that says "a threefold cord is not quickly broken" (Ecclesiastes 4:12) and these three cords (commitment, sacrifice and faith) come to mind. I believe that executing them as a country would be very beneficial towards preserving our unity. Obviously, this will take individual and collective effort by those who are truly aware of what is at stake and are willing to bear the infirmities of the less informed. Commitment, sacrifice and faith are what unity is all about. This country has stood on these principles along with God's favor for more than two centuries.

Many times, we hear talk about politicians and their real and or perceived lack of loyalty to those they serve. But one good thing that I can say about our country is that the usual response of an American politician (when he or she is defeated), especially on the state and federal level, is to ask the voters to unite with them to support the incumbent for the benefit of all. Yet while many politicians verbalize this idea, it is expedient that we begin to function in this manner if we are to be a truly successful society.

So, in this year, in these times, it is crucial to support our current president and his staff to help elevate our country to magnificent horizons. We have experienced a lot of painful and frustrating events over the past few years but if we could perhaps believe what the singer Betty Wright says or what many bodybuilders say when they say "no pain…no gain", then we must be moving in the direction of gain. Someone once said "It's always darkest before the dawn" and America is moving towards that light and the execution of our core principle of unity can and will lead to success if we remember…United we will stand to seek life, liberty and the pursuit of happiness if we trust in God.

Allif Dove
Revised September 2011

* * *

XII

12. Hope

hope
noun

**A feeling of expectation and desire for a certain
thing to happen.**

Principle: Hope

From Problems to Progress to Productivity

(Let's Make It Happen America!)

America's current dilemma might prompt William Shakespeare to say "To get healthy or not to get healthy! That is the question!" There use to be a question we would ask each other in my inner city neighborhood years ago. Somebody in a group would ask, "If a robber came to you waving a gun and said give me your money or your life, what would you say?" Oftentimes someone younger and materialistic would say "my life." Most of us knew giving our life more value than money was wiser so we would argue that point. As we look around our country and see our young dying and/or getting sick at alarming rates, it's obvious that seeking money, prosperity and things is the unanimous choice while our very lives are being jeopardized. Congress reportedly remains divided on the health care issue largely due to cost disputes, yet it is apparent that the mental and physical health of our society desperately needs to be addressed properly. I would venture to say most Americans have sat in funeral services and wondered if accessible health care, including preventive medicine and early diagnosis, could have given our dearly departed friend or relative a better chance to live. Therefore, we can ask ourselves at this critical juncture in American history, as we review our record of helping other societies, should we insist on choosing life over money and if so how can we work out a feasible solution. To arrive at a desirable destination concerning this issue requires an overview of what has happened, a consideration of what is at stake, a realization of the source of indifference involved and an earnest desire to advance from problem to progress to productivity.

A quick scan over our American history would reveal that the 1940's and 1950's were periods during which putting emphasis on forming and maintaining a typical family structure was a high priority. As a result, healthy living, including eating right, seeking education and getting good health care at home and from the doctor, was a routine practice. Since then, wars, epidemics like crack cocaine and methamphetamines and the rise in serious illnesses like AIDS, cancer, diabetes, depression and bipolar disorder have resulted in massive mental and physical illness. As a result, professional accessible health care is clearly needed for all. If we don't address this need, we will be choosing money over life. In the movie "I am Legend" actor Will Smith gave us a picture of how life could be if no one else lived. In the Bible we are told in Proverbs 4:7 that "Wisdom is the principal thing; therefore, get wisdom, and in all your getting get understanding". Our country, by virtue of apathy, poor choices and violent criminal action, is sick and wellness is truly needed. Who, for example, has a very good and productive day at work when they are sick? This scenario gets worse when there is uncertainty about what one can do to get better. Let's be real today and acknowledge we do have many working-class people who are under insured or have no health care at all.

When we consider what is at stake in this phase of our national recovery it is clearly evident that the medical industry has been and continues to rake in record profits. In addition, the lack of a sense of security about whether you can be treated, should illness occur, is fearful for any rational person. Our country, in the advanced civilized state we are in, can find a way to ensure medical treatment for all while promoting wellness by emphasizing education about and action toward healthier living. Surely this idea presents a challenge especially in the areas of administration and finance to ensure that government dollars go toward good service at the most economical rate. An important element of this management would be to determine when recipients have achieved a better quality of life and no longer need this option. And as we wisely consider what route to take, let us remember our national security is affected by all issues. Although the American way seriously guards individual freedom and choice, when it comes to our overall well being, whatever we decide to do will take our collective best.

Our choices seem to be in discussion everywhere we turn. Tune in your television or radio, log in on your computer or open a newspaper and you will hear about one or both of two conflicting viewpoints. In general, one viewpoint says handle your own dilemma and the other speaks more of caring for and sharing with others. While we are all entitled to our own opinion, it should be noted that where two conflicting viewpoints exist together, division arises making destruction inevitable. The Holy Bible says it like this in Matthew 12:25 " Every kingdom divided against itself is brought to desolation; and every city or house divided against itself shall not stand". With this in mind, how do we begin to address and correct our conflicting viewpoints in order that we might establish one conviction (to help or not to help) thereby ending our division and enhancing our chance to stand together. Although all societal issues matter, at the core of this one rest where we really stand as a nation of people, and of greater significance determining which forces drive our decisions dictating our outcomes. Our current status is a result of past decisions to trust elected officials and corporate America to conduct our affairs.

It is apparent we have come up on another providential moment in our American history. During this opportunistic time of determining what route is best we can be assured that protesters will protest, bloggers will blog, analysts will analyze, conservatives will be conservative and liberals will be liberal. We will continue to have tea parties and town hall meetings. At times the police may have to restore order but this is much better than civil war. As it now stands our public safety and welfare truly still hang in the balance.

Amid our debate about national health care let us remember that last November we were so fed up with the efforts of our president, who many felt was unworthy of public approval that we intensely scrutinized each candidate for president, picking the one who thoroughly expressed how he planned to work for our restoration. Around the same time, we began to find that

145

corporate America had many overpaid CEOs who proved to be incompetent opportunist. Company after company reported disastrous conditions which we are still feeling the impact of today.

With this in mind it is now time to gauge whether or not our public executives (Representatives and Senators) are working for the success of our society. If we don't, they may well drive us into a worse state by bickering instead of examining proposals, explaining them to their constituents and voting in the special interest of our society. It is their job to do this and it's our job to make sure they do their jobs. After all, a system must be checked periodically to see if it is working as it should be. We have been going in the wrong direction for a while, yet by the grace of God we are still afloat. The health care debate is really a no-brainer. With mental and physical illness growing at alarming rates this is becoming an issue of national defense. Sickness is no respecter of person and our future depends on what we do today. So, can we stay focused, work together, and seize this opportunity to ensure that these executives, who are empowered by us, actually work in our best interest by passing needed bills that work? After all, which one of us appreciates receiving anything counterfeit?

Allif H. Dove
September 2, 2009.

Since this commentary was written we know the Supreme Court of the United States of America voted to uphold the health care bill of 2012 as being constitutional. And since it is constitutional let's get on with the business of developing a healthy society. Besides, if we rebound economically and digress physically and mentally, we won't have the quality of life to enjoy it. The final two commentaries (Deeply rooted in the American dream) is committed to the idea of putting our differences aside (with regard to race, color, creed, sex, or anything that separates us) and working for a better American society and (There is hope) speaks to the idea that each of us can play a vital role in gaining a true and lasting recovery by seeking God who is the true hope.

* * *

Deeply Rooted In the American Dream

For an African-American citizen in today's society there must exist a double mind. It's hard not to think about the state of our nation but on the other hand it's hard to avoid thinking of how the ancestral evolution of African-Americans has and continues to develop so poorly overall. When we view both entities, we can't help but notice the apparent likenesses. First and foremost, noticeable is the affluence of some Americans both African in origin and non-African in origin. The wealth of some of these individuals is so vast and far above the average citizen it is astounding. Second, the means by which this affluence is attained is also easily noticeable and in some ways very troublesome. Exploitation is so apparent these days it's almost scary. And third there continues to be a lack of an ability of the exploited classes of both of these entities to form, stand and work together. You may wonder, "Where are you going with this idea?" Well, I can best tell you by revisiting a famous dream.

Reverend Dr. Martin Luther King Jr. once told of a dream he had. Most people from that era and who study history know in this dream he saw equality and fairness. He saw mutual respect and caring concern for our fellow man. Reverend King spoke from a standpoint of personal awareness of mistreatment of a people, a quality and exhaustive education (PHD) and arguably and most importantly an immense spiritual development. The things Reverend King accomplished on earth in 39 short years are still acknowledged and appreciated today. And one of these many noteworthy legacies he demonstrated (not devised) was the importance of taking a courageous, unified stand, with the hope and purpose of developing a peaceful, productive and joyous society. His dream was that African-Americans, who at the time were grossly discriminated against, would be able to receive dignified treatment and an unhindered opportunity to live, learn and enjoy life.

The "American Dream" could be summarized as the ability to experience "Life, liberty and the pursuit of happiness." And Reverend King felt based on his dream we would one day experience a country where people will be judged not by the color of their skin, but by the content of their character. In essence we could derive that Reverend King envisioned that a person should have the ability, regardless of personal (origin/race/color) appearance, to experience life freely and to seek happiness. This idea coming from a highly spiritual and educated man, who realized that suppression and oppression by nature were damaging this country as well as the world, sounds good but how can it be accomplished?

Reverend King saw our solutions as rooted in love. This love, demonstrated at times as passive and submissive (non-violence), was actually responsible and courageous. He encouraged the type of love that would spot, examine and positively address areas that need improvement. Love that would always compel a man or woman to always look in the mirror first to avoid bringing a negative judgment on themselves, their family, this country and especially on God.

The Reverend Dr. Martin Luther King Jr. had a dream that he said was "deeply rooted in the American dream." Today the rich are richer than ever (money wise that is). They use every media, communications and information systems outlet possible to send messages that tend to result in suppression and oppression of everyday people. And the everyday people focus on getting out of the barrel, but for lack of unity and unadulterated goodwill towards each other, they keep pulling each other down and never getting to the solution. I believe Reverend King knew that the spirit of suppression and oppression results in more anger, violence and depression which leads to more crime, addiction, sickness, imprisonment and death. I also think he knew the only way to avoid the disastrous course we were on would be to love by exposing the problem (boycott, marches), addressing the problem (speeches, legal steps, education) and trusting almighty God to produce the desired change.

Today as we consider our direction and our potential fate we must ask ourselves some serious and pertinent questions. Where would America be if Africans were not shipped here? How would the industries and economy of America have developed without Africans who were taken from their land? What would have become of all the inventions, methods, ideas, art and entertainment supplied by Africans, which contributed to the development of America? We could also pause here and consider that with African descendants America is what it is but we don't know what it would be without Africans (one could only speculate). What we do know is that God permitted this union of Blacks and Whites. And although what we have here today is okay; it is slowly deteriorating because we can't or won't get along. A man named Rodney King, after being beaten for evading the police, became well known years ago for saying "Why can't we all just get along?"

If Reverend Dr. Martin Luther King Jr.s' dream is connected to God's hope for us to treat each other right (regardless of race, sex, political affiliation, etc) and get along, we can begin by asking for His help. Then focus on seeking His guidance and knocking down any door that prohibits us from experiencing love, peace and harmony as we enjoy life and liberty while pursuing happiness.

Allif Dove
August 14, 2010

* * *

There Is Hope

In society today there seems to be so much chaos, corruption and violence. It appears that family values continue to deteriorate, the education system is in a state of disarray, politicians can't be trusted, and children are underdeveloped and misguided. We see fits of rage, violent attacks and unbelievable episodes that if they were not so troublesome and detrimental to the idea of human decency, would be hilarious. Yet in the light of all of this, which is only topped by the virtual ease at which some people are able to execute a thought to take another life, there is hope.

You may wonder how one envisions hope in what seems a hopeless situation. Well, the word of God says in Isaiah 55:8 "for my thoughts are not your thoughts, neither are your ways my ways." Thus, when the natural man or woman (thinking their way) views the news, instantly fear arises, which of course is natural. But when the spiritual man or woman (whose hope and trust are in God) views the same news, although it may be troubling and disturbing, they quickly remember their trust in God who says in Isaiah 40:10 "Fear thou not; for I am with thee: be not dismayed." If you are able to believe nothing happens in this world apart from God's divine permission, he will provide you peace, comfort, clarity and yes hope.

This hope is available to all who seek it but unfortunately many people today don't know how to believe while others have lost their belief. Let me first say that before a new belief can be developed or re-established one must be convinced that their way does not work. The Bible states in Luke 15:17, that after leaving home to live life his way the Prodigal Son concluded "And when he came to himself, he said, how many hired servants of my father's house have bread enough and to spare and I perish with hunger. His condition made him willing to discord his thoughts and ways and believe again in his Father's way. Releasing his way, which ceased to work, made him capable of believing.

After we are willing to believe in Almighty God, we must believe in the one God sent to help us (see John 6:29). Knowing Jesus, the Word, is how our faith will grow. In today's society our faith is the only neutralizer to the fearful messages sent through the news. A few years ago, I experienced the power of faith. The day my mother-in- law, Ruthie Lee Taylor, passed away I sat in the hospital talking with my wife and sister-in-law (while mother clung to life). My sister-in-law explained how a few days earlier when mother appeared to be recovering, they were discussing plans for when her mother returns home from the hospital. As they talked, mother interjected this thought "I might not come home…. but any way it goes it will be alright!" Hallelujah, Praise God! Now that was faith in action. When you know, believe and trust God, you understand everything will be alright.

Remember that though the situation seems hopeless there is hope in God. Renew or establish your faith today. And if you have strayed or are lost or in doubt, renewing your faith today will be the best decision you can make.

Allif Dove
December 4, 2010

* * *

Conclusion

As I reflect on the last words of the Star Spangled Banner, "For the Land of the Free, and the Home of the Brave", the implications that come from these words are very profound. The description is of an America where the people are free and also brave. If we ask several people about freedom and bravery there would be countless and far-ranging replies. But can we really deny the potential for freedom available in this country. Likewise, the many brave acts in, around and outside of this country by our brave citizens throughout the years are hard to overlook. The idea of freedom and courage are in reality only ideas unless put into practice.

In this book I have shared some ideas about our state of affairs and like many things these ideas are debatable. What is not debatable is the state of our country. The war amongst us continues to frustrate our ability to truly progress. As with any serious illness or a major crisis the response should be definite and thorough. Thus, if we realize, remember and consistently react to the truth of our condition, I feel confident that we can't and won't go wrong.

Liberties are earned. Liberties must be maintained with purposeful efforts. They are to be enjoyed, appreciated and safe guarded as the precious benefits that they are. The blessing of God and the ideas that our great country has been founded upon are highly responsible for our success and happiness in this country over the years. Our actions, especially in government (over a period of time), had been, and in some cases still are, largely irresponsible or lackluster at best and seem to be largely responsible for our state today. In spite of the fact that many of our citizens today believe that "God blesses America, our home sweet home" and they don't like the current conditions, they may not truly realize the importance of putting forth our collective, determined and committed best effort to come out of our condition. The holy bible says "Faith without works is dead" and we should "Love our neighbors as ourselves", so if we commit to putting these two ideas in motion we will be actually functioning like the U-NI-TED States of America, which, by the way, is who we are.

Allif Dove
An American Writer

* * *

About the Author

Elder Allif H. Dove serves in Christian Ministry as the Coordinator of the Life Recovery Support Group at San Francisco Temple Christian Assembly Church. He is a published American Writer, residing with his wife Linda, in St. Louis, Missouri. A Father of seven adult children and a lover of people, he has labored many years as a Human Services professional, serving in various capacities helping others, to include Addictions Counselor, Case Manager and a Group Facilitator.

Elder Dove lives with the belief that, "because God gave His only begotten son, Jesus, for us, that we should, in return, surrender our lives to God and serve God with all that is within us."